Presented by Create and Blossom

# Creating by Faith

## 6-Day Bible Study to Enhance Your Writing Journey

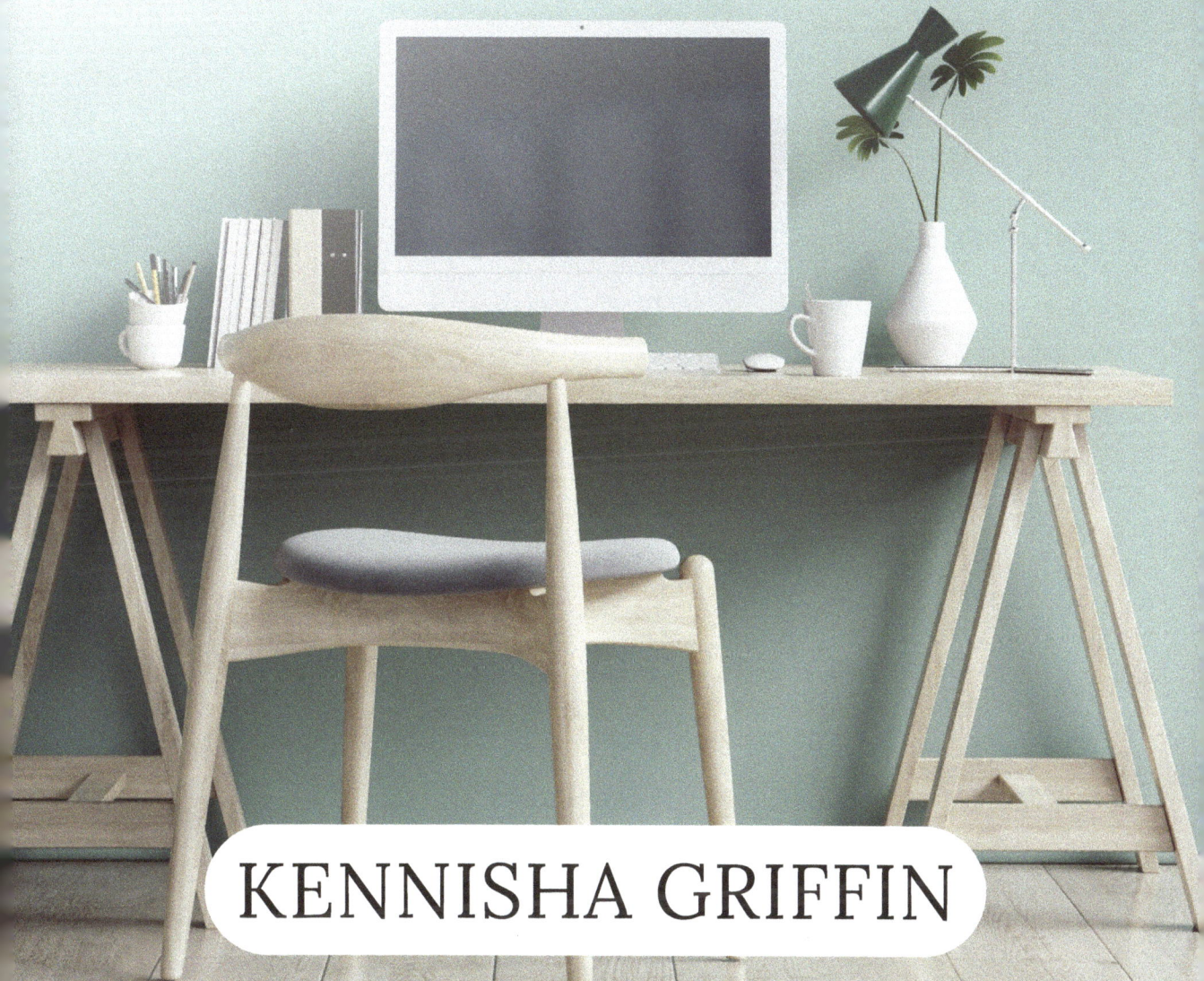

## KENNISHA GRIFFIN

*Creating by Faith*
**6-Day Bible Study to Enhance Your Writing Journey**

Published by Create and Blossom
712 Austin Avenue
Waco, TX 76701
www.createandblossomstudios.com

*Images and AI use by permission of Canva.*
ISBN: 978-1-945304-65-1 paperback
ISBN: 978-1-945304-61-3 hardcover
ISBN: 978-1-945304-63-7 eBook

Printed in the United States of America

First Edition

CREATE & BLOSSOM
LITERARY STUDIOS

# Table of Contents

INTRODUCTION

# Hello, I'm your coach Kennisha Griffin.

Thank you for downloading *Creating by Faith*. This project is close to my heart as it encapsulates the essence of why I started Create and Blossom. My goal is to support writers in sharing stories of faith, hope, and love, as well as to mentor and guide aspiring authors on their path to publication.

This Bible Study is designed as a weekly tool for reflection. As writers, we encounter numerous challenges and often require reminders of our calling, enthusiasm, and divine purpose. I hope this inspires you to continue honing your writing skills and using your words to offer hope and inspiration to others.

Grab a cup of coffee or tea, join me, and together, let's delve into how God's word can support us in our path as writers and authors.

— *Kennisha Griffin*

WWW.KENNISHAGRIFFIN.COM

Embracing this journey requires faith, perseverance, and a deep understanding of our God-given talents.

LESSON 1

# Embracing your Creative Journey

## Introduction

As authors, we often find ourselves navigating through the peaks and valleys of the creative process. Our journey is filled with moments of inspiration, bouts of writer's block, and everything in between. Embracing this journey requires faith, perseverance, and a deep understanding of our God-given talents. Through the lens of Scripture, we can find guidance and encouragement to fuel our creative pursuits.

To ground our discussion, let's consider several passages from the Bible about creativity.

## Scripture Focus:

1. **Genesis 1:1-3:** "In the beginning, God created the heavens and the earth. Now the earth was formless and empty, darkness was over the surface of the deep, and the Spirit of God was hovering over the waters. And God said, 'Let there be light,' and there was light."
2. **Exodus 35:31-32:** "And He has filled him with the Spirit of God, with wisdom, with understanding, with knowledge and with all kinds of skills—to make artistic designs for work in gold, silver, and bronze."
3. **2 Timothy 1:6-7:** "For this reason I remind you to fan into flame the gift of God, which is in you through the laying on of my hands. For the Spirit God gave us does not make us timid, but gives us power, love, and self-discipline."

LESSON 1 CONTINUED

**The Divine Act of Creation (Genesis 1:1-3):**
The very first act recorded in the Bible is one of *creation*. God's creation of the heavens and the earth from a formless void is a profound reminder of the power of *creativity*. As authors, we are called to mirror this divine creativity by bringing our stories, characters, and worlds into existence.

**God-Given Talents (Exodus 35:31-32):**
The passage highlights Bezalel, whom God filled with His Spirit, granting him wisdom, understanding, and artistic skills. Similarly, each one of us has been endowed with unique talents that are meant to be used for a higher purpose. Consider your own writing skills as gifts from God.

**Fanning the Flame (2 Timothy 1:6-7):**
Paul's encouragement to Timothy to "fan into flame the gift of God" serves as an important reminder to nurture and develop our creative gifts. The journey of writing can sometimes be daunting, filled with self-doubt and fear. However, the spirit given to us is one of power, love, and self-discipline.

PRACTICAL APPLICATION

**Reflect on how the act of writing is your participation in the ongoing act of creation.**

**How can you hone your talents and use them to serve others and glorify Him?**

**Reflect on ways you can overcome obstacles in your creative journey and stay committed to your craft.**

We can create narratives that not only entertain but also uplift and glorify God.

LESSON 2

# Writing with Purpose and Passion

## Introduction

Writing with purpose and passion transforms our stories into powerful vessels of faith and inspiration. By committing our work to the Lord, infusing our words with heartfelt passion, and trusting in His plan, we can create narratives that not only entertain but also uplift and glorify God. Let us pray for guidance, strength, and creativity as we continue our writing journeys, always keeping the heart of our stories rooted in His love.

## Scripture Focus:

1. **Proverbs 16:3**: "Commit to the Lord whatever you do, and he will establish your plans."
2. **Colossians 3:23**: "Whatever you do, work at it with all your heart, as working for the Lord, not for human masters."
3. **Jeremiah 29:11**: "For I know the plans I have for you," declares the Lord, "plans to prosper you and not to harm you, plans to give you hope and a future."

LESSON 2 CONTINUED

### Writing with Purpose (Proverbs 16:3):

The heart of any compelling story lies in its purpose. As authors, we must ask ourselves why we write. In Proverbs 16:3, we are reminded to commit our endeavors to the Lord. This commitment means seeking His guidance and ensuring that our writing aligns with His will. By doing so, our stories can serve a greater purpose, whether it's to inspire, educate, or offer comfort. Reflect on your writing goals and consider how they align with your faith. Are you writing to glorify God and uplift others? Let your purpose be your guiding light.

### Infusing Passion into Your Words (Colossians 3:23):

Passion is the driving force that breathes life into our stories. Just as God's love for humanity is evident in every page of the Bible, our love for the craft should shine through our writing. Colossians 3:23 (NIV) tells us, "Whatever you do, work at it with all your heart, as working for the Lord, not for human masters." When we write with all our heart, our passion becomes contagious, capturing the hearts of our readers. Take time to reflect on what ignites your passion for writing. Let that fire fuel your creativity and dedication.

### Trusting in God's Plan for Your Writing Journey:

Paul's encouragement to Timothy to "fan into flame the gift of God" serves as an important reminder to nurture and develop our creative gifts. The journey of writing can sometimes be daunting, filled with self-doubt and fear. However, the spirit given to us is one of power, love, and self-discipline. Reflect on ways you can overcome obstacles in your creative journey and stay committed to your craft.

PRACTICAL APPLICATION

**How do you define the purpose behind your writing? How can you ensure it aligns with your faith?**

**What specific aspects of your writing are fueled by your passion? How can you cultivate this passion further?**

**Can you share a time when you faced a challenge in your writing journey? How did your faith help you overcome it?**

Authors can create characters that embody compassion and reflect God's love.

LESSON 3

# Reflecting God's Love in Your Creations

## Introduction

As authors, we hold the unique ability to breathe life into characters and weave narratives that resonate with readers. But beyond entertaining, literature can also be a powerful medium to reflect deeper truths and values. One such value is compassion, a cornerstone of God's love. This study aims to explore how authors can create characters that embody compassion and reflect God's love.

To ground our discussion, let's consider several passages from the Bible that highlight compassion:

**Scripture Focus:**

1. **Matthew 9:36 -** "When he saw the crowds, he had compassion on them because they were harassed and helpless, like sheep without a shepherd."
2. **Ephesians 4:32 -** "Be kind and compassionate to one another, forgiving each other, just as in Christ God forgave you."
3. **Colossians 3:12 -** "Therefore, as God's chosen people, holy and dearly loved, clothe yourselves with compassion, kindness, humility, gentleness and patience."

LESSON 3 CONT.

**Understanding Motivation:**
Characters who exhibit compassion often have a deep understanding of others'
pain and struggles. As an author, delve into your characters' backstories to find
what drives their empathy. Perhaps they have experienced loss or hardship
themselves, or they've been mentored by someone who modeled compassion.

**Demonstrating Actions:**
Compassionate characters are defined by their actions. Use pivotal scenes to
showcase how your characters respond to others in need. Whether it's a small
act of kindness or a significant sacrifice, these moments can profoundly impact
your narrative and your readers.

**Growth and Transformation:**
Not all characters start as compassionate individuals. A powerful story arc can
involve a character learning to embrace compassion. This transformation can be
inspired by their experiences, relationships, or even divine intervention,
mirroring the transformative power of God's love in our own lives.

PRACTICAL APPLICATION

*Characters that embody God's love should be relatable, displaying a mix of strengths and vulnerabilities. This relatability allows readers to see themselves in the characters' journeys and inspires them to reflect similar values in their own lives.*

**Can you name a character from a book or movie who embodies compassion? What makes their compassion believable and impactful?**

*While it's important for characters to have aspirational qualities, they should also be realistic. Perfect characters can seem unattainable, whereas those who struggle and grow in their compassion are more inspiring and believable.*

**How can you incorporate more compassion into your current writing project?**

*Subtly weave moral lessons about love and compassion into your story. Avoid preachiness; instead, let the characters' actions naturally convey these messages. This approach can lead to more profound and lasting impressions on your readers.*

**Reflect on a time when you experienced God's compassion. How might that experience inform your writing?**

We can find strength and encouragement in God's Word.

;LESSON 4

# Perseverance in Publishing

## Introduction

As authors, we often face countless challenges on our journey to publication. Whether it's dealing with writer's block, rejection letters, or self-doubt, the path to seeing our work in print can seem daunting. However, as followers of Christ, we can find strength and encouragement in God's Word. This study aims to explore the biblical principles of perseverance and trusting in God's perfect timing, providing spiritual nourishment for your writing journey.

To ground our discussion, let's consider several passages from the Bible that highlight trusting in God's timing:

**Scripture Focus:**

1. **Galatians 6:9:** "And let us not grow weary of doing good, for in due season we will reap if we do not give up."
2. **Proverbs 3:5-6:** "Trust in the LORD with all your heart, and lean not on your own understanding; in all your ways submit to Him, and He will make your paths straight."
3. **Ecclesiastes 3:1:** "For everything there is a season, and a time for every matter under heaven."

LESSON 4 CONT.

### The Call to Perseverance

Galatians 6:9 reminds us that perseverance is essential in our endeavors. As authors, the act of writing is a form of doing good, a creative expression that can inspire, educate, and uplift others. The verse encourages us not to grow weary, promising that our hard work will bear fruit in its due season. Reflect on your writing process.

### Trusting God's Timing

Proverbs 3:5-6 teaches us to trust in the Lord and not rely solely on our own understanding. This is crucial for authors, as it's easy to become discouraged when our timelines don't align with our expectations. Instead, we are called to submit our plans and ambitions to God, trusting that He will guide our paths.

### Embracing the Seasons

Ecclesiastes 3:1 highlights that there is a season for everything, including the season of waiting. This can be a time of growth, learning, and spiritual development. Sometimes, delays and setbacks are opportunities for God to prepare us for greater things. Reflect on a season of waiting in your life.

PRACTICAL APPLICATION

**What challenges have you faced? How can you draw strength from this promise to keep pushing forward?**

**Consider the times in your writing journey when things didn't go as planned. How can you practice trusting God more fully with your writing career?**

**Reflect on a season of waiting in your life. How did it ultimately benefit you? How can you view your current season with a perspective of faith and anticipation for God's perfect timing?**

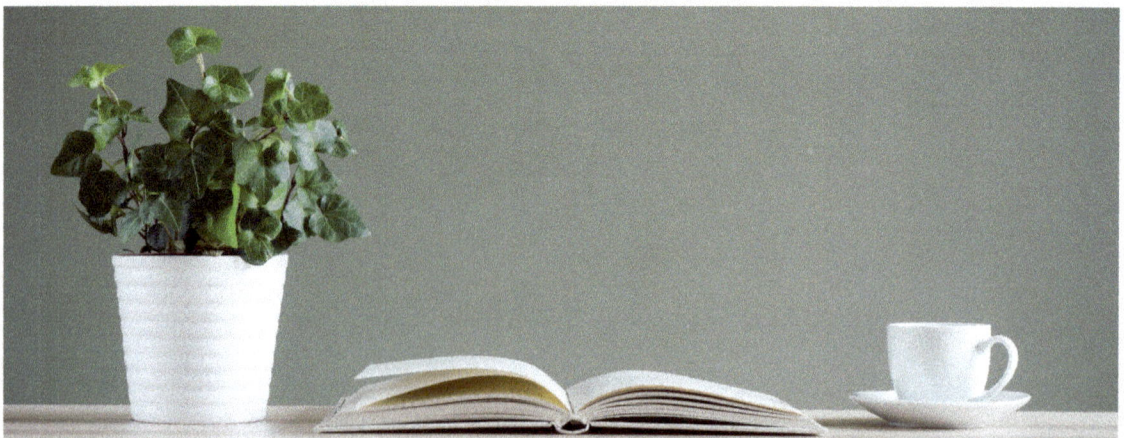

We can have meaningful collaborations, shared wisdom, and mutual encouragement.

LESSON 5

# Community and Collaboration

## Introduction

Writing is often perceived as a solitary activity, but it doesn't have to be. The Bible encourages believers to find strength and support in community. For authors, this can translate into meaningful collaborations, shared wisdom, and mutual encouragement. In this study, we will explore biblical principles of community and collaboration, and how these can be applied to the writing journey.

To ground our discussion, let's consider several passages from the Bible that highlight finding strength in fellowship:

## Scripture Focus:

1. **Ecclesiastes 4:9-12 (NIV)** "Two are better than one because they have a good return for their labor: If either of them falls down, one can help the other up. But pity anyone who falls and has no one to help them up. Also, if two lie down together, they will keep warm. But how can one keep warm alone? Though one may be overpowered, two can defend themselves. A cord of three strands is not quickly broken."
2. **1 Corinthians 12:12-14 (NIV)** "Just as a body, though one, has many parts, but all its many parts form one body, so it is with Christ. For we were all baptized by one Spirit so as to form one body—whether Jews or Gentiles, slave or free—and we were all given the one Spirit to drink. Even so the body is not made up of one part but of many."
3. **Hebrews 10:24-25 (NIV)** "And let us consider how we may spur one another on toward love and good deeds, not giving up meeting together, as some are in the habit of doing, but encouraging one another—and all the more as you see the Day approaching."

LESSON 5 CONT.

**The Benefits of Collaboration:**
Ecclesiastes 4:9-12 highlights the practical benefits of working together. Authors can draw from this wisdom by recognizing that collaboration can enhance creativity and productivity. Whether it's co-authoring a book, participating in a critique group, or simply sharing ideas with fellow writers, the synergy of working together can lead to greater accomplishments and a sense of shared achievement.

**The Body of Christ Analogy:**
In 1 Corinthians 12:12-14, Paul describes the church as a body with many parts, each with its own role and function. Similarly, the writing community is diverse, with each author bringing unique skills and perspectives. Embracing this diversity can lead to richer, more varied storytelling. Writers can learn from each other's strengths and support each other's weaknesses, creating a more vibrant literary community.

**Encouragement and Accountability:**
Hebrews 10:24-25 emphasizes the importance of encouragement and meeting together. For authors, this could mean forming or joining writing groups, attending workshops, or engaging in online forums. Regular interaction with other writers can provide the motivation needed to persevere through challenges, celebrate successes, and maintain accountability in writing goals.

PRACTICAL APPLICATION

**Form a Writing Group:** If you're not already part of one, consider starting or joining a local or online writing group. These groups can offer critique, encouragement, and accountability. *Share your experience with a writing group.*

**Collaborate on Projects:** Look for opportunities to co-author a book, write guest posts for each other's blogs, or contribute to anthologies. Collaboration can introduce you to new audiences and fresh ideas. *Share your experience collaborating on a project.*

**Share Resources:** Exchange books, articles, and other resources that can help fellow writers grow. Share your expertise and be open to learning from others. *In what ways are you resourceful?*

We can find inspiration and rediscover the flow of creativity that God has placed within us.

LESSON 6

# Overcoming Writer's Block- Faith in the Flow

### Introduction

Writer's block can be an overwhelming obstacle, leaving authors feeling frustrated and creatively stifled. This Bible study aims to provide spiritual encouragement and practical guidance, rooted in faith, to help authors navigate and overcome writer's block. By leaning on scriptural wisdom, we can find inspiration and rediscover the flow of creativity that God has placed within us.

To ground our discussion, let's consider several passages from the Bible that highlight faith in the flow.

### Scripture Focus:

1. **Philippians 4:13:** "I can do all things through Christ who strengthens me."
2. **Proverbs 3:5-6:** "Trust in the Lord with all your heart and lean not on your own understanding; in all your ways submit to him, and he will make your paths straight."
3. **Colossians 3:23:** "Whatever you do, work at it with all your heart, as working for the Lord, not for human masters."

LESSON 6 CONT.

**Acknowledging the Block:**
Begin by acknowledging the writer's block and the frustration it brings. It's important to remember that even biblical figures faced seasons of waiting and uncertainty. Reflect on Philippians 4:13, which reminds us that through Christ's strength, we can overcome any obstacle, including writer's block. This verse encourages us to depend on God's strength rather than our own.

**Trusting God's Timing:**
Proverbs 3:5-6 teaches us to trust in the Lord and lean not on our own understanding. Writer's block may be a period where God is teaching us patience and reliance on Him. When we submit our writing process to God, He can provide clarity and direction. It's essential to trust that God's timing is perfect, and He will guide our creative flow when we place our faith in Him.

**Writing as Worship:**
Colossians 3:23 reminds us to approach our work with a heart dedicated to the Lord. Writing can be an act of worship, a way to glorify God through our creativity. By shifting our focus from the pressure to produce to the joy of creating for God's glory, we can find renewed motivation and passion. Consider setting aside time for prayer and reflection before writing sessions, inviting the Holy Spirit to inspire and guide your words.

PRACTICAL APPLICATION

**Prayer and Meditation: Start your writing sessions with prayer, asking God to bless your time and creativity. Meditate on the scriptures mentioned to ground yourself in faith.**

**Journaling: Keep a journal to document your thoughts, prayers, and any inspiration that comes to you. This can help break through mental barriers and spark new ideas.**

**Community Support: Connect with other Christian writers for encouragement and accountability. Sharing your struggles and triumphs with others can provide new perspectives and motivation.**

# God is with you

*"So do not fear, for I am with you; do not be dismayed, for I am your God. I will strengthen you and help you; I will uphold you with My righteous right hand" – Isaiah 41:10*

My sincere hope is that this bible study has uplifted and empowered you with the motivation and an inspiring message necessary to continue writing and produce books that ignite transformation. As writers, we hold a remarkable chance to utilize our talents as a means of ministry to guide numerous individuals in finding the hope found in Christ and the resilience He offers to progress positively.

I recommend keeping this study accessible as an ebook for quick reference on your phone or tablet, on your coffee table, or in your office. Combine it with a beloved journal or notebook, and respond to a question sincerely each day. This practice will boost your faith and inspire you to keep making a positive impact in the world.

— *Kennisha Griffin*

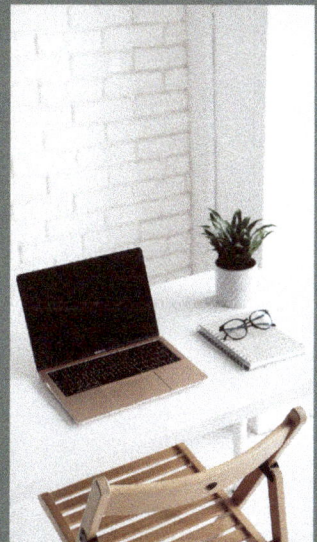

www.ingramcontent.com/pod-product-compliance
Lightning Source LLC
Chambersburg PA
CBHW042337030426
42335CB00028B/3368